The Art of
Active
Listening

*How to Listen Effectively in 10 Simple
Steps to Improve Relationships and
Increase Productivity*

Richard Banks

Thank You!

Thank you for your purchase.

I am dedicated to making the most enriching and informational content. I hope it meets your expectations and you gain a lot from it.

Your comments and feedback are important to me because they help me to provide the best material possible. So, if you have any questions or concerns, please email me at <u>richardbanks.books@gmail.com</u>.

Again, thank you for your purchase.

INTRODUCTION

"We have two ears and one mouth so that we can listen twice as much as we speak." —Epictetus

If you need to improve your relationships and professional productivity, this is the book for you.

You're likely already aware of the importance of good communications skills. What many people don't realize, however, is that the key to successful communication isn't about talking at all. Effective communication hinges on learning how to listen actively. Poor listening breaks down communication faster than you might imagine and creates rifts that are sometimes impossible to heal.

With this book, my goal is to give you a solid grasp of the processes involved in listening well to help you improve your communication skills and, as a result, your relationships.

While active listening is often referenced in professional contexts, it's just as crucial in personal relationships. You're happiest and most successful when you understand and are understood by those around you. This mutual understanding, however, is only possible through ongoing, quality communication.

In these pages, we've broken down the complexities of active listening into 10 easy-to-learn steps. By practicing and implementing the practical strategies to accomplish each of these steps, you'll learn to:

- Train your attention
- Listen with purpose and empathy
- Advance your leadership ability
- Present diverse ideas in your conversations
- Develop healthy relationships

As you cultivate a deep-listening mindset, you'll begin to facilitate more meaningful conversations, and these interactions lead to even greater benefits. Improving your ability to communicate effectively eases and encourages the exchange of ideas. In addition to saving time that would otherwise be wasted on misunderstanding and repeated attempts at clarification, you open the door to creativity and innovation.

These chapters will guide you through assessing your listening skills, establishing clear goals for yourself, confronting barriers to your ability to listen actively, and, ultimately, developing healthy, lifelong habits of effective communication. This begins by delving into exactly how listening plays into the dynamics of communication. As we investigate the psychology involved in active listening and how it's reflected in relationships, you'll see this is especially clear as we explore the challenges that arise when people don't listen.

You'll discover how definitive evidence from numerous recent psychological studies informed and molded this 10-step approach. We'll dig into the psychological principles at work when communication breaks down, which results in accumulating tension, frustration, and even fractures in relationships. Even more critically, we'll examine how to avoid these pitfalls and transform strained, ineffective communication into clear and effective exchanges of information and emotional understanding through thoughtful listening.

My goal is to help you improve your deep listening skills in measurable ways so you can achieve quality results. I want to help you strengthen relationships and inspire those around you, which will have a profound impact on your personal productivity and happiness. You'll learn the significance of:

- Giving accurate feedback
- Encouraging participation
- Minimizing misunderstanding
- Clearly grasping the motives of others
- Acknowledging and empathizing with other perspectives

In addition to providing a simple template for rating your listening skills, each chapter focuses on one critical element involved in deep listening. If your impulse is to think that just listening can't possibly involve 10, separate, essential components, you've come to the right place! Listening may sound like a simple concept, but so much is involved in listening well to achieve true understanding. In fact, the inability to truly listen is actively destructive to relationships, eroding trust and compassion.

If you want to be a better leader, friend, and partner, following these 10 steps can help you get there.

Of course, instituting change takes work. Developing new habits of thought and behavior takes time and focused effort, even after identifying current harmful patterns and determining how to correct them. Incorporating practices of healthy listening into your everyday interactions is well worth the effort! You'll see the impact in every aspect of your life, personal and professional.

So, if you're ready to dramatically improve your

productivity and interpersonal relationships, let's get started!

CHAPTER 1: THE KEY TO EFFECTIVE COMMUNICATION AND SUCCESSFUL RELATIONSHIPS

"We are stronger when we listen, and smarter when we share." – Rania Al-Abdullah

It's easy to say effective communication is essential. What's more challenging is understanding the many interconnected elements involved each time we communicate. Each aspect of communication comes with the potential to exert either positive or negative influence. How these factors interact and impact your communication, specifically, hinges on how well you understand and apply them.

The Dynamics of Communication

We often refer to "dynamics" when talking about communication, but what does this really mean? At its core, communication is a dynamic process. This simply means that communication is, by definition, constantly changing. This makes sense. When you talk to someone, the experience is an interactive, fluid process, with each person choosing their words based on what the other says.

You can't have a complete conversation by yourself because a monologue is missing this critical interactive element, and you have no external influence to which you can respond. Instead, words run in a straight line from beginning to end, following the path of your thoughts. There are reasons creativity results from multiple minds engaging a problem together; the line of thinking is pushed and pulled in new and unfamiliar directions.

As humans, language is our primary means of expressing ourselves. Even sign language uses a slightly different medium (actions instead of words) to perform the same function (Houston 2014). While certain languages are tonal, and most include some variation of the written word, all of us require a medium through which to interact. We use language to articulate our internal experiences and thoughts and to respond to experiences shared by others. While we communicate through language, more is involved in the process than just the words we select.

Just think for a moment about the challenges inherent in multi-lingual situations—literally referred to as language barriers. Failure to understand blocks communication. Speech is essentially useless for the purposes of communication unless it's being received. Essentially, it's impossible to communicate without understanding and internalizing what's being said. This is where listening comes in.

A Two-Way Street

Complex communication involves much more than words, of course. We take in visual, verbal, and nonverbal cues every time we interact with another person. You likely aren't surprised to learn that active listening depends upon being receptive to all these complexities. This is, in fact, one of the primary challenges and sources of misunderstanding in so many newer forms of digital communication. Have you ever had a text misunderstood, for instance, because your intended tone failed to translate to the other person? Ever wondered what inspired the creation of emoticons? That's right—our need to pair visual cues with verbal ones.

Logically, it makes sense that communication "goes both ways," as the saying goes. Talking with one other person is merely the simplest form of basic communication. The complexities of verbal and nonverbal cues grow exponentially for each new person introduced into an interaction. Part of becoming a more effective leader depends on your ability to remain aware of and interpret even the most complex team dynamics.

One of our aims in the following chapters is to improve your leadership skills by showing you how you can stay attuned to the many elements at play every time your professional team interacts with you and with each other. Just consider how often meetings are derailed by an individual who's "not on the same page" as the rest of the team, or how an interpersonal conflict reverberates and causes distraction and disruption.

Following this path of communication beyond work interactions leads directly into personal relationships. Here, communication is, if anything, more critical to maintaining empathy and understanding. If you want to connect deeply with people, you must be able to comprehend them deeply.

When your emotional investment is heightened, it's challenging to remain receptive to what someone is trying to communicate. Your own thoughts and emotions, understandably, tend to get in the way. In our urgency to express our feelings and experiences, our focus shifts away from the other person, and we stop listening. Developing active-listening habits that facilitate deep communication is a core component of maintaining healthy relationships, personal and professional. Deeper listening results in deeper relationships in immediate and direct ways.

Good vs Bad Communication Skills

While our intent isn't to make anyone feel judged, it's important to be aware of the areas where your ability to communicate effectively falls short. None of us is a perfect communicator. Odds are, you're reading this book because you're aware of this and want to improve your communication ability. You're in good company. When we stop wanting to learn and grow, we stagnate. This is a journey and, with the right tools, we learn and improve every day.

Poor communication quickly creates mistrust and confusion in any relationship. Therefore, it's critical to remain attuned to signs that communication is suffering before the effects cause permanent damage to your relationships. Though communication requires more than one person, when communication breaks down, it's common to see a few specific elements and habits in at least one individual:

- Interrupting or talking over the other person
- Being distracted/multitasking during conversations

- Qualifying statements, accusations, and false apologies or excuses for communication failure
- One-way communication
- Negativity and a passive-aggressive attitude
- Invalidating feelings, assuming, or claiming someone else's experiences
- Making it personal (This is relevant for both professional and personal relationships.)
- Making universal statements (generalization)
- Avoidance—indirect engagement and avoiding eye contact
- Self-absorption or keeping responses and opinions in your head
- Not asking questions
- Mind-reading or stereotyping
- Maintaining unrealistic expectations
- Using harsh words
- Dishonesty
- Failing to articulate positives
- Disengaging emotionally or physically from the conversation

Don't worry; we're all guilty of these communication shortcomings. What's important is acknowledging that we have room for improvement and choosing to make changes!

By the end of this book, you'll have gained new confidence in your communication skills and continual growth. In addition, I hope you'll understand better how to encourage others to continue pursuing their journey toward excellent communication.

The Psychology of Listening

Listening is more than the physical processes involved in hearing and processing sounds or visual cues with our brains. This external stimulus must be interpreted before it has meaning (Tennant 2021). To wrap your mind around this, think about the phenomenon known as "spacing out." In the midst of a conversation or halfway through a movie, we suddenly realize we've become absorbed in our thoughts and have no idea what was just said, or we stare at the screen without comprehending what's happening. We've all done this. Technically, our ears are still hearing the sounds, but, without our attention, they're meaningless.

There are plenty of things that can cause a breakdown in our active processing of these external stimuli. Even simple exhaustion can impede our ability to listen. This is one reason that timing your critical conversations is just as important as actually having them. Entering a heavy or emotional conversation when you aren't prepared to listen usually won't turn out well.

Current Theory

Active listening—sometimes called deep listening—is all about attention. Specifically, it's a psychological term that refers to a form of focused, intentional processing of auditory stimuli that involves more than just passively hearing words as they're spoken (Remijn 2010). Active listening requires engaging consciously with all aspects of communication—verbal and nonverbal—and demonstrating this participation through various techniques like reflecting and questioning, which we'll investigate later.

Humans are social creatures, so it makes sense that any skills that reinforce our ability to work together define our relationships with one another. In short, the connection facilitated by listening is a fundamental human need because it enables us to interact and understand each other. Unfortunately, this doesn't mean our body will communicate to us when we fail to listen effectively, the way it communicates hunger when it needs fuel. Listening is a skill we must cultivate through practice, practice, practice. Only when you're familiar with the indicators and habits of ineffective listening will you be able to catch yourself and correct them.

Therapeutic and Practical Applications

According to the American Psychological Association, active listening has been proven to be so effective that it's the psychotherapeutic technique at the foundation of client-centered therapy (Bodie 2015). Psychologists employ active listening as a strategy to help ensure that their clients are getting the most out of therapy sessions. This technique helps ensure a therapist accurately understands clients to the greatest extent possible.

Of course, it's impossible to experience the reality of being another person or having their exact experiences, thoughts, and feelings. However, we can gain a greater understanding of others by optimizing our listening ability. For this reason, active listening is also a technique commonly taught to clients in many types of relationship therapy, such as couples therapy (Angera 2006). Relationships simply can't survive without effective communication, and that communication is impossible without listening. It's also notable that the concept of therapy to heal emotional wounds and broken communication is built upon active listening. After all, problems must be understood before they can be appropriately treated.

Outside of formal therapy, the concepts of active listening can be applied to all types of communication with similar benefits. That said, it's much easier to retrain yourself to develop healthy listening habits by starting with a more formal approach and narrowing your application of listening techniques to specific interactions. Sustained focus takes energy, even more so when your mind isn't used to it. Fortunately, our minds can be retrained, and, once learned, the habits we learn tend to stick until we intentionally change them. Once these habits become more natural, you'll be able to integrate active listening into all aspects of communication in your life and realize the benefits for years to come.

The Impact of Listening on Relationships

In some ways, it's funny that we feel the need to distinguish between personal and professional relationships when talking about communication because both of these types of relationships require the same level of clear communication and active listening to thrive. In fact, all our human interactions necessitate effective communication.

Of course, the degree of emotional involvement is what distinguishes the personal from the professional category. In a professional environment, being open about deeply personal experiences and emotions is inappropriate, but this honesty is essential (in varying degrees) to healthy personal relationships. As you can likely already tell by the various qualifiers, all relationships are complex and unique, no matter their category.

Each of these two categories requires its own form of

24

honest communication, but these different standards don't make one type of communication easier than the other. Listening is just as critical in professional interactions as it is in personal ones. Though the content of your communication is different, the listening techniques you apply to achieve understanding are identical. Both personal and professional relationships require establishing clear expectations and respect through active listening.

Challenges When People Don't Listen

When you fail to give another person your full attention, for whatever reason, you're communicating that you don't value—or, at the very least, you undervalue—the time and attention that they're giving you. You are, in essence, telling someone that you don't value them.

If this sounds extreme, consider the last time someone you were speaking with was distracted, maybe by an ongoing text conversation or another interaction nearby. How did losing their attention make you feel? Did you get the sense that they cared about the story you were telling them or the message you were trying to communicate? Probably not. The loss of attention and interest might have made you feel insecure or hurt, perhaps even angry. Generally, the more significant the content of what you're telling someone, the more intense your reaction when you feel the other person isn't listening or the communication is otherwise undermined. While distractions happen all the time—and are, in fact, unavoidable—how we manage communication around distractions and other disruptions communicates how we value not only that information but also that individual.

The various barriers to listening can cause different forms of conflict and communication breakdowns. Some obstacles to good communication can make people feel slighted and cause personal hurt, while others result in misunderstandings that can disrupt projects and undermine trust. Depending on your profession, breakdowns in listening can cascade into life-threatening situations. Multiple studies have examined how the healthcare field is negatively impacted by ineffective listening and communication (Jahromi 2016). Whether between medical professionals or healthcare providers and patients, this communication breakdown is never a good thing and can have serious repercussions.

For each step of the active-listening process in the following chapters, we'll provide a specific example of how listening behavior directly impacts communication. Ultimately, we'll demonstrate how your choices about your listening behavior and attention result in either good- or bad-quality communication.

CHAPTER 2: THE POWER OF ACTIVE LISTENING

"The most important thing in communication is hearing what isn't said." – Peter Drucker

What Is Active Listening?

Active listening, as its name suggests, refers to actively listening—fully concentrating on what's being said rather than just passively hearing the speaker's message. Active listening is the ability to focus entirely on a speaker, understand their message, comprehend the information, and respond thoughtfully. Active listeners use verbal and nonverbal techniques to show and keep their attention on the speaker. This supports your ability to focus and helps ensure the speaker can see that you're focused and engaged.

While there are specific steps you can take to develop habits of active listening, these skills must be adapted to each situation. Learning when and how to apply active-listening skills is just as important as learning the skills themselves.

Benefits of Active Listening

By now, you're likely beginning to grasp how active listening can dramatically impact your interactions. Improving your ability to empathize and problem-solve has implications that will cascade through your relationships and productivity into every aspect of your life. But let's consider some of the specific benefits of practicing active listening:

- Establish and reinforce trust
- Demonstrate concern
- Develop sensitivity to nonverbal cues
- Communicate respect
- Avoid miscommunication

- Get complete information
- Connect over shared experiences
- Affirm experiences
- Retain information
- Manage emotional conflict

Because active listening encourages you to better understand the other person's perspective and empathize with it, relationships benefit. While this applies in all day-to-day activities, it becomes even more critical in times of stress and conflict.

In a workplace or educational setting, active listening enables you to be a better collaborator and learner because it helps you better understand the other individuals involved. In interviews, active-listening skills are invaluable, too. After all, in order to provide a complete answer to any question, you must be confident that you fully understand the question and have all the relevant details and information required to form an appropriate response.

In any interaction, active listening reinforces habits of patience. By truly focusing on what the other person is communicating to you, you sublimate your urge to interrupt or speak over them. As a result, getting to know new people and expand your social network is easier for active listeners. It also tends to be easier for more naturally patient individuals to internalize the various steps involved in active listening. We're not saying you must be patient to listen; we're saying you might need to put in a bit of extra effort if patience doesn't come naturally to you.

Four Goals of Listening

Generally, we listen to accomplish four primary goals. We listen:

1) To obtain information
2) To understand information or people
3) For enjoyment
4) To learn

Each of these elements is important to living a happy, productive life. Individuals who grow up with limited or absent interpersonal communication skills suffer from the loss for the rest of their lives. While we can obtain information and learn in solitude, studies show that we retain and internalize information better through interactions with other people (Canpolat 2015). Even actively listening to recorded music gives us opportunities to share experiences and emotions.

Barriers to Effective Listening

Before we can implement the techniques involved in listening well, we must first remove those habits that block our ability to listen. Note that the list below isn't comprehensive; there's no way it could be. While there are hundreds of variations on barriers that disrupt our ability to listen well, they're easily categorized by common habits, including:

Interrupting or Changing the Subject

Talking over someone tells that person that you value your thoughts and ideas more than theirs. In most cultures, this also conveys a direct lack of respect for the person. Even if you disagree or have an emotional response to what someone is saying, it's important to remember that how you choose to say something is just as meaningful as what you say. Besides, when you're speaking, you're not listening. As much as we enjoy believing in our multitasking prowess, it's impossible to do both simultaneously—or, at least, not well.

Rushing

Similarly, rushing someone to complete a thought indicates you value your time over theirs. If they consider what they have to say worth the time to say it, you must respect that. There are, of course, exceptions and emergencies. Use your judgment. However, if you genuinely don't have time for a conversation, you can simply request to have the conversation at a time when you can give the speaker your full attention. This courtesy itself indicates respect for the individual and their ideas.

Avoiding Eye Contact

Maintaining eye contact (keep in mind that we're not talking about actually staring!) keeps our attention focused on the person speaking. A lot of this involves how the human mind processes information based on how our bodies are constructed. Consider the shape and placement of your ears. They're designed to primarily amplify sounds coming from directly in front of us. Where we direct our field of view is where we'll pick up sounds most effectively. Listening, in effect, comes down to both anatomy and psychology. Consider situations when someone actively avoids making eye contact with you. Generally, this tells you they're uncomfortable in some way. Perhaps something else is holding their attention more than you are. They may even be lying.

Relying on digital communication and avoiding face-to-face interactions increases the odds of miscommunication and, in some cases, feels outright dismissive. Nonverbal cues convey a lot about how someone is feeling and how well they're receiving information. It also makes it easier to ask prompting questions based on cues like hesitation or other indicators of uncertainty. If you can make time for a face-to-face interaction, do so. Emoticons can, at the end of the day, only communicate so much. The hundreds of muscles in the human face do a much better job.

Rabbit-trailing

Rabbit-trailing is the term used when we choose to focus on a single detail of what someone has said simply because it interests or upsets us. Doing this distracts us from the larger point of what they were attempting to say. In professional settings, especially, this wastes a significant amount of time, decreases productivity, and creates unnecessary frustration. It's important to consider the context of your communication as a key component of your listening. In an informal, social setting, rabbit-trailing might be a means of sharing and bonding—but it could also cause frustration, particularly if it becomes a regular habit.

Dismissing or Joking

Humor has its place in healthy interactions, but it's inappropriate if used to belittle another person or their ideas or even if it simply distracts from a point a person is making. Sarcastic or cutting remarks not only detract from what a person is saying but they also undermine respect for that person. A shared inside joke with another person in a group setting is equally damaging because it creates subdivisions within the group dynamics on top of other problems. Being dismissive, in any way, conveys a lack of respect and prevents you from learning.

Waiting

You might be thinking, "Isn't waiting for the other person to finish speaking before I do a good thing?" While patience is critical to effective listening, focusing on the thought or response in your mind while waiting for them to finish speaking isn't patience, it's selfishness. Is your moment of insight or anecdote so important that it's worth failing to process the rest of what a person is saying? Of course, this barrier is situational. In general, however, if a point is worth making, your mind will prompt you to bring it up again later.

Waiting includes cases of listening with a goal already in mind. When you engage in a conversation designed to lead the other person toward a specific outcome, you won't actually be listening at all. You'll be strategizing and distracted from what they're saying. This is a common bad habit people tend to fall into in supervisory roles. Remember, you can communicate your end goal to the other person up front or choose to wait until after you've listened to them to move in that direction. If you're truly listening to what your colleague is saying, you may discover an entirely new solution you wouldn't have come up with on your own. Effective listening involves forcing your own opinions about what should or shouldn't happen to sometimes take a back seat. Be open to new perspectives and experiences.

Disengaging

This can involve everything from emotionally shutting down from a conversation to just spacing out. If you need a break from an emotional interaction, it's important to communicate this and continue the conversation later when you're prepared to engage actively. If your mind is wandering because you're exhausted, the same principle applies. Communicate how you feel so the other person doesn't take your inattention as a reflection of your opinion of them or their ideas. If you catch yourself avoiding eye contact, this is a helpful indication that you may be disengaging from what someone is saying.

Judging

This is a tricky barrier to avoid because all humans have opinions. However, judging is about more than having your own opinions; it's about projecting them

38

onto another person. Judging can be communicated in many ways. Even if you say nothing, your body language is revealing. Moreover, once you've passed judgment on a person or idea, you shut down the possibility of viewing them or their idea in any other way. You stop listening because you've already decided how you feel about what they're saying. This often occurs when people allow stereotypes to cloud their thinking or come to a snap judgment based on a pet peeve triggered by something inherent in the other person or something they said.

Disagreeing with what someone has said isn't a good reason to stop listening to them. If anything, it's a reason to listen more deeply and attempt to understand their point of view, especially if you want them to return this courtesy.

Getting Distracted

Distractions are perhaps the most significant barrier to effective listening because they're often unavoidable. While many people can sustain high-quality listening for a short period, distractions can quickly derail even effective communication and make it difficult to get back on track.

Developing new habits that support active listening involves making choices and changing behaviors long before you're in a listening situation. For example, suppose you're engaging in a planned interaction, a sit-down dinner, or a one-on-one meeting. Even if the setting is informal, you can choose to silence your cell phone and select an environment in advance that will be conducive to connecting effectively. For different situations, this might look different. For example, date night will be far more effective when you're facing one another across a table in a quiet restaurant rather than sitting at the restaurant bar side by side. Fit the venue to the interaction and plan how you can minimize distractions in advance. In an office setting, you might have your calls held, for instance.

Often, our own thoughts are what distract us. Regular meditation or mindfulness practices have been shown to be effective in this regard. Create a set time in the morning during which you focus your mind on examining and releasing thoughts that might otherwise intrude and distract you during the day.

Another method is to write down a nagging thought or concern so your mind doesn't feel the acute need to hold onto it throughout the day. If journaling and mindfulness aren't for you, look into other strategies that might help you tackle distraction. Even cutting out stimulants like caffeine might help.

Listening Habits

Our listening habits develop over time. Some are neutral, but most lean toward the positive or the negative based on their impact on our ability to communicate well. It's essential to first identify your negative listening habits so you can catch them as they occur and replace them with positive listening habits.

Of course, habits, by definition, are so familiar to us that they're unconscious. It's often difficult to notice—much less correct—habitual behaviors. This is where support comes in. It's worth telling at least one person you trust that you're working on correcting a specific behavior and asking for their help. When they notice you slipping back into the negative habit, they can alert you (ideally immediately, but sometimes it's necessary to wait for a more private setting). Just remember not to chastise them for doing as you requested! It's not easy to be called out on our failings.

Identify Negative Listening Habits

To help you identify your negative listening habits, begin by rereading this list of examples. Certain patterns or situations will likely feel uncomfortably familiar.

- Interrupting
- Rushing
- Avoiding eye contact
- Rabbit-trailing
- Dismissing or joking
- Waiting
- Disengaging
- Getting distracted

Recall a few of your recent conversations. Did you engage in some of these bad habits? If so, which ones? Be honest with yourself. You likely succumbed to more than one. You may even slip into all of them occasionally. That's why you're reading this book now, to figure out how to change those habits into better ones!

Another good approach is to ask a trusted friend whether they've noticed any of these habits recurring when you're listening to them. Try not to be defensive when they tell you. Family members are often best at calling out negative listening habits because they've experienced them the longest and are less likely to rationalize them on our behalf. They may also leap at the opportunity to be, to put it kindly, helpfully judgmental. Remind them to be kind, too!

Develop Positive Listening Habits

One of the most effective ways to address negative listening habits and correct them is by directly replacing them with positive habits. In the following chapters, we'll dig into these habits and why they're effective tools to promote active listening. Each of these tools is broken down into manageable steps, but keep in mind that there isn't a set pattern to actively listening. Each step is interconnected with the rest.

Ideally, each of these elements is at work every time you listen. Identifying specific steps that will help you counter your current habits is a great place to start, but it's easy to get overwhelmed. Begin by focusing on replacing one bad listening habit with a single active-listening step. Each time you catch yourself slipping back into that habit, stop and think through what you're doing and why. You may even consider asking the person speaking to give you a moment to collect your thoughts so you don't stop listening in the meantime.

CHAPTER 3: STEP 1 – FOCUS YOUR ATTENTION

At least once in our childhood, we can all recall being told to focus. Unfortunately, focusing is easier said than done, but there are strategies that can help. Remember, before you can begin to develop positive habits of attention, it's important to remove negative ones that will disrupt your ability to focus.

Remove Distractions

Distractions are the most common disrupter of active listening. Part of the reason is that some distractions and interruptions are beyond our control. As they say, stuff happens. In these situations, it's crucial to plan how you'll address a distraction that pulls your attention away from what someone is saying. Thinking through potential distraction scenarios helps prepare you for the moments when they inevitably happen. With preparation, you can equip yourself with specific responses and avoid, as much as possible, being caught unprepared.

For example, imagine you're listening to a friend while walking to the local park, and someone else you know (but who's unfamiliar to your friend) comes up and interrupts your conversation. Which is a less rude response—to stop listening and greet the new arrival or to ignore the interloper and continue listening?

It's a tough call. Impulsively, in that moment, what would you do? In practice, most of us would break off listening and greet the newcomer. While there's nothing inherently wrong with this response, it's important to think through what this behavior communicates to the friend who'd been speaking to you.

Is there a way to disengage from the first conversation to address the interruption that conveys that you still want to listen to what they're saying? Absolutely! Think through and articulate a few specific responses. Repeat them to yourself in a mirror, or perhaps in the shower or the car, until they come quickly to mind. The next time an unexpected interruption occurs, you should be better prepared.

However, remember to follow through on what you say, or the loss of attention will be compounded by your failure to keep your word. If you told your friend, "Hold that thought for a moment. I don't want to miss the rest of the story," make sure you prompt them to continue once the interruption is over. Also, be certain to return your complete attention to them. Interruptions tend to fracture concentration beyond a single moment.

This is just one example. There are nearly unlimited potential distractions beyond your control, so focus on some of the more common ones that you experience. Consider acting out a few situations with a family member or friend if you're having difficulty envisioning your response in the moment. The more work you do in advance, the better listener you'll become.

Other distractions are well within our control, and these tend to be more insidious. The distractions we allow to occur are generally behaviors we want to engage in or that provide some type of positive reinforcement. For example, we interrupt someone to take a phone call from a friend. A common distraction is to text intermittently during an in-person conversation.

Generally, the person already engaging you in conversation should take priority, no matter the closeness of their relationship to you. If you're on the phone with someone, focus on completing that call and listening with your full attention to what's being said before engaging in another interaction. It's more meaningful for each person to have your full attention than for both to get only partial engagement from you. Your split attention communicates a lack of interest and respect.

Be Present

Once you begin correcting your negative habits, you can focus on enhancing positive ones—specifically, focusing your entire attention in the moment, also known as being present. It's interesting how often our physical selves can be present when our mind is entirely elsewhere.

You may be disengaging intentionally or simply allowing your thoughts to wander while listening. As discussed in the previous chapter, intentional disengagement often involves emotional distress of some kind. Give yourself permission—and give the other person the respect—to stop a conversation rather than allowing it to continue one-sided. Ask to resume the conversation when you're prepared to be fully engaged. Depending on the situation, you might need to be more or less firm with your request for a hiatus.

Far more common is becoming lost in our own thoughts or inner monologue. Addressing this issue requires developing the skill of silence. If this sounds intimidating, it's likely because silence is so unfamiliar to most people's everyday experience.

Healthy habits are a little different for each of us because health looks a little different for each individual. What works to clear someone else's mind might not work for you. Some people swear by yoga or meditation practices. Others set aside daily time to engage in mindfulness. Some people go on walks.

If you're struggling to keep your attention on the person talking to you, you might try picturing your attention as though it has a physical form—like a beam of light that projects from your mind or eyes, for instance. This makes it easier to catch and redirect that beam when it begins to wander. While this may feel odd at first, practice and repetition are the only way to create new habits. Whatever you do to focus, try to spend some time thinking about your attention and what it means to engage it fully.

The myth of successful multitasking is precisely that, a myth. While it's possible to engage in multiple tasks simultaneously, this requires splitting your attention and, in the end, giving no task the benefit of your complete focus. It helps to remind yourself why you're making this effort to focus your attention—to improve your listening skills and, thus, improve your relationships and productivity.

Divided attention is, in many ways, worse than no attention. When you present yourself as engaged in listening—through words or actions—it's vital that you actually *are* engaged. If not, you are, in effect, lying. It makes sense that someone would feel betrayed if they discovered partway through speaking to you that you haven't retained the information they gave you. By beginning that interaction, you entered an informal social contract, intentionally or not. How you choose to handle that contract is your responsibility. Will you put in the time and effort to read the fine print and discover the unexpected, or are you going to skim?

It's worth noting that anyone dealing with an attention disorder is already at a disadvantage when it comes to focusing their attention. If this applies to you, medical professionals are often the best resource for determining additional strategies to help you improve your focus.

Practical Tips

For many people, sustaining focus is one of the most challenging aspects of active listening. We've created some practical exercises and pointers for anyone struggling with maintaining attention to make the job a little easier. As you begin practicing, keep in mind that the more frequently you use your new active-listening skills, the faster they'll solidify into a habit.

Choose the strategy that most easily fits your lifestyle and schedule; the easier an exercise is to implement, the more likely you are to keep doing it.

List and Dismiss Distractions

Before beginning a conversation, ask the other person to give you one minute to clear your thoughts. Sit or stand, whichever is most comfortable for you. Mentally walk through each thing that draws your attention as you wait. This might be anything from the weather outside to a rattling fan to the smell of your coworker's lunch to your own mental to-do list. One at a time, hold these distractions in your mind and think about dismissing them. At the end of the minute, hold the person who's about to speak in your thoughts. Then, begin your conversation.

Mark Your Calendar or Create a Checklist

At least once a day for the next three weeks, schedule yourself to actively listen to someone or something for at least five minutes. This might be a friend or even a podcast. Ensure that nothing else is scheduled during this time.

Exercise

Studies show that exercise can improve your ability to focus. Create a simple workout routine based on the times or situations when you most need to use your active-listening skills. One good method for making it easier to focus is to increase your heart rate for at least 20 minutes within an hour or two of when you must begin focusing your attention.

Shut Down Digital Distractions

Turn away from or turn off screens and alert sounds whenever you're about to enter a conversation.

Meditate

Meditation is an excellent means of silencing your thoughts. To perform a simple meditation, sit somewhere comfortable. Clasp your fingers gently together in your lap. Close your eyes. Inhale a deep breath through your nose and exhale slowly through your mouth. As you exhale, relax your body. Think about your breathing. Focus on the air filling and leaving your lungs and nothing else. As thoughts occur to you, let them drift away. Continue to breathe evenly for 15 minutes.

CHAPTER 4: STEP 2 – SHOW THAT YOU'RE LISTENING

The old adage "actions speak louder than words" exists for a reason. Listening to someone benefits both of you much less if that individual isn't sure they have your full attention. When someone believes you're disengaged, they're less likely to engage themselves fully, and your mutual communication is likely to fracture and be far less productive.

Acknowledge the Speaker

Showing you're listening begins with acknowledging the speaker. This can be as simple as saying their name or addressing them by their official title. The appropriate acknowledgment will vary with the situation. It may also include a question, such as, "Do you have something you want to talk to me about?" But why is this acknowledgment so important? Consider the following example:

Your coworker walks into your office. You begin asking them about a project, and both of you speak about that for a while. Eventually, you realize you're almost late for a meeting and apologize that you have to cut your conversation short. Your coworker tells you not to worry about it, and both of you go your separate ways. What went wrong? Did you catch it?

Even though you didn't intend to, you left no room for your coworker to voice the question they originally came to your office to ask. Even when you're on friendly terms—perhaps you're friends outside of work—you allowed your assumption that they'd speak up if the matter was important to give yourself permission to dominate the conversation. You may not have meant to, but you prioritized what you had to say over what the other person had to say. You didn't show listening behavior.

Listening begins when you stop and focus your attention on another person, even if they haven't begun speaking yet. By acknowledging them, you communicate that you value them enough to want to hear if they have something to say. They may not, but, either way, you've displayed that you respect their ideas. You give them time to reorient themselves for a conversation and organize their thoughts without immediately responding to you. You're providing an opening for the other person to speak. You also remind yourself to listen with this technique. Acknowledging is a good habit for prompting you to focus your full attention and prepare to listen.

Acknowledging shouldn't be restricted to the beginnings of conversations, either. Whenever a person begins speaking, you should acknowledge that it's their turn, rather like passing an invisible "talking stick." Your acknowledgment need not even be audible. You can communicate a lot simply through body language and redirecting your attention. However, it will probably help you to say or do something to indicate you've begun listening.

Pay Attention to Body Language

Even if you have no formal training in reading body language, certain behaviors, gestures, and postures convey specific attitudes or "read" a certain way. We communicate more nonverbally, in terms of emotion, than we do with words. Just think about how much is communicated by a simple glance.

As someone is speaking, part of focusing your attention means paying close attention to both what their words and their body tell you. If someone's shoulders are hunched, they may feel intimidated or upset. If their arms are crossed, they might feel defensive. Facial expressions are part of this. Sometimes, someone's words and what their body conveys doesn't align. This is when it's most important to pay attention to body language and part of why giving someone your undivided attention is so critical. You won't know what questions to ask if you miss half of what's being (nonverbally) said.

While reading body language is essential, you need to find a balance. You don't want to become so absorbed in reading body cues that you fail to listen to what someone says. In general, you can use pauses or gaps in the conversation to check if body language has changed significantly. Fortunately, our minds process much of this information naturally. The more you focus your attention on body-language communication, the more natural it will become and the less you'll need to concentrate on sensing how someone is feeling as you listen to them.

Provide Nonverbal Signals

As you listen, it's important to continue to provide the speaker with clear signals that they continue to have your attention. Just as you're reading their body language, they're reading yours.

Consider how much the person you're listening to is communicating nonverbally. They're picking up even more from your nonverbal signals when you're listening because they don't have verbal ones. It's important to maintain:

- Positive body language
- Signals of interest
- Eye contact

Positive body language is, generally, anything that communicates openness and alertness. Sitting up, turning to face a person, and uncrossed arms are all positive indicators. Signals of interest include still fingers, thoughtful and attentive expressions, and minimal fidgeting. Most of all, eye contact communicates where your attention is.

This doesn't mean staring; in fact, staring communicates hostility—exactly the opposite of what you want to convey when actively listening. While you, as the listener, will occasionally glance away or gaze into the middle distance as you search for thoughts, remember to bring your eyes and attention back to the speaker. It will tell them you're listening, and it's not a bad reminder for you, too.

Practical Tips

Showing someone that you're listening can feel quite uncomfortable at first. You may feel hyper-aware of your body language and how you might be distracting the person who's speaking. The best way to overcome this discomfort is to practice a few simple exercises until this body language becomes a habit.

Creating new habits takes time, of course. However, the more often you can practice, the quicker you'll be able to stop focusing on how you're communicating that you're listening and, instead, just focus on listening.

Practice in a Mirror

Stand or sit in a chair in front of a mirror so you can see most of your body in the reflection. Ideally, the mirror will be full-length and from three to four feet in front of you. Now, practice a few attentive postures. Lean slightly forward, just enough to shift your weight without becoming uncomfortable. Tilt your head slightly forward or to one side. Make eye contact with your reflection. Furrow your brow slightly to indicate concentration. Nod slowly. Keep your arms held loosely at your sides or have your hands in your lap. Keep your legs parallel or slightly open, not crossed. Repeat these postures in front of the mirror for 10 minutes a day for the next three weeks.

Focus on Separate Facial Features

This is an excellent exercise for anyone who struggles with maintaining eye contact without staring. When you speak to someone, focus on their facial features one at a time. Start with their eyes, if it's comfortable for you. If not, choose another feature first. As the person is speaking to you, slowly shift your gaze among the different features of their face. Over time, incorporate more sustained eye contact. This exercise will keep your gaze resting on the person speaking and communicate your attention while helping you become increasingly comfortable maintaining casual eye contact.

People-Watch

Though it might sound silly, the next time you're sitting in public, such as at a restaurant or on a bus, do some people-watching. Look at how people sit when they're relaxed and comfortable. Pay attention to how they arrange their limbs and move their arms when speaking. Try to identify people who seem defensive or closed off, and think about how specific aspects of their posture and body language telegraph this impression. This will help your brain reinforce the link between the posture and psychology.

CHAPTER 5: STEP 3 – LISTEN TO UNDERSTAND

Listen for Intent

When someone is speaking, it's easy to latch onto specific terms or phrases—or even whole sentences—and choose to interpret them literally. Misreading body language plays into this. It's crucial that you listen to try to understand what the person wants to communicate, which can be (and often is) much more than just the literal interpretation of the words they say.

Taking Things Literally

Deep listening involves more interpretation than just understanding what a sentence tells you. You must apply your full attention to determine the complete message. Specifically, this is an area where judgment can be a serious pitfall. It's tempting to use someone's actual words to judge them or their ideas, consciously or subconsciously, so challenging those judgments and assumptions is crucial for effective communication.

For example, if someone asks you to sit down because they want to talk to you "about your rude language," it might be tempting to latch onto the word "rude" to counter the points they try to make. You might say their judgment of what they consider rude shouldn't dictate your personal language choices. While convenient for you—because it means you won't have to consider your behavior more deeply or think about why someone is receiving your language as rude—this is a way of avoiding acknowledging the intent behind the words.

You're choosing to allow yourself that word choice to reinforce a judgment you want to make because it allows you to dismiss the person's argument rather than addressing it seriously. This is a common defensive tactic, and our brains tend to jump past our reasoning to come to our defense, so it's important to be aware and combat this tendency.

While listening to what someone is saying is essential, deep listening requires hearing what they intend to say rather than just the superficial communication of words. This is also a great opportunity to challenge your tendencies toward judgment. If you find yourself being dismissive because of the way someone speaks— for example, because of their accent or speech patterns—this indicates a negative listening habit.

Mind-Reading

Clinging to literal interpretations also occurs when people engage in mind-reading. In other words, when you imagine what another person is thinking and act as though that imagined intent is their actual intent, you're failing to listen. You are, instead, hearing what you want to hear. You may discover you've even been trying to lead the conversation in a specific direction, and this imagined intent is a convenient way to get you there guilt-free.

As in all aspects of active listening, it's important to challenge your own biases and negative or self-serving habits. When your whole focus is truly on the other person, however, this becomes much easier.

Form a Mental Picture

A tried-and-true strategy for maintaining sustained attention is to form a mental picture of what's being described. For anyone whose attention tends to wander, this is often a great solution. You're able to engage your brain at several levels, so if you find yourself getting easily bored when someone is long-winded, consider practicing this technique.

Be careful, however. It's easy to slip from forming mental pictures that keep you engaged in listening into tangential, wandering images. This technique will work better for some than for others. If you already have a tendency to daydream or "space out" when someone else is speaking, it's probably a good idea to keep looking for another strategy to help you listen for intent.

More practically, if someone is describing a physical location or interaction, creating a mental picture improves your ability to follow what they're saying and, as we'll discover, ask the appropriate questions to get complete information or "fill out" that picture.

Listen to Content and Context

To ensure you're getting the complete picture, remember to consider both the content—the words—and the context of someone's speech. Depending on the situation, this can mean several things. It might mean remembering they had a couple of margaritas with dinner, for instance, that are probably influencing their tendency to be more flippant about a serious issue than they'd normally be. They might have had a trying or stressful day. They might even be distracted by something outside your conversation.

Considering context might even involve the physical location where a conversation is occurring. Conversations held inside hospitals, even about mundane topics, are often more loaded or weighty than conversations that happen elsewhere. As humans, we often have emotional associations with particular locations; that's why coming up with the appropriate setting for date night is so tricky. For a first date, you want to set a certain tone, whereas, for a years-long relationship, you're likely interested in another atmosphere altogether.

You should also consider how the presence of other people (including you) is directly impacting what someone is saying. Communication can't happen in a void, and all communication is influenced by the people engaging in it. Even as a listener—perhaps especially as a listener—you influence what's being said and how it's being said.

For instance, if someone is aware that a certain subject might be sensitive for you because of a past experience you've had, they'll alter the way they reference that subject. You need to be aware of the many influences at work. That said, it's impossible to live inside another person's head and understand the exact influences on their thinking and the precise context of their words.

All you can do is your best. That is, you can choose to focus your entire attention on determining as much as you can about the forces acting on someone's words as you listen to them. The more you can figure out, the better listener you'll become.

Practical Tips

This step can seem particularly challenging because there aren't physical behaviors to practice in the same way as with some of the other steps. Even though listening to understand is more abstract, there are a few mental exercises that can help you retrain your brain to pay closer attention to the content of what someone is telling you and how they feel about what they're saying.

Though we've already discussed how to create a mental picture to help you concentrate and expand your understanding of what someone is saying to you, there are several other simple exercises you can practice that will help improve your understanding when listening.

Create Summaries after Conversations

For the next several weeks, keep a notebook with you

or create a note on your phone dedicated to conversation summaries. At the end of each conversation during this time, write down a summary of it. Depending on the duration of the conversation, the length of your summary will vary. However, it will likely be between two and ten sentences long. This exercise trains your mind to pay closer attention to and work to better understand what someone is saying in the moment to better recall the content later to create a summary.

Look for Discrepancies

As someone is speaking, check for two separate elements involved in what they're saying. First, consider the content of their words and the message those words are creating. Second, consider their body language, tone, and attitude. Finally, think about whether these two elements match one another. If not, ask yourself why; if you don't understand why, you might ask the person to explain the disparity.

Consider the Other Party

Each time the person speaking brings up another person in any way, try to picture that individual. Think about what you know about that person and how that information matches up with—or conflicts with—what's being said. Not only will this help prompt you to ask better questions to understand any conflict between these two elements, but it will keep you more aware of how this information interacts with its context, the physical world around you, and the people involved.

A Short Message from the Author

Hi, are you enjoying the book thus far? I'd love to hear your thoughts! Many readers do not know how hard reviews are to come by, and how much they help an author.

I would be incredibly thankful if you could take just 60 seconds to write a brief review on Amazon, even if it's just a few sentences!

Thank you for taking the time to share your thoughts!

CHAPTER 6: STEP 4 – LISTEN WITH EMPATHY

Empathy refers to your ability to understand and share the feelings of someone else—in this case, the feelings of the person you're listening to. While perfect empathy—a complete understanding and sharing of feelings—is impossible, active listening is the best way we have to approach this kind of connection.

Equating our experience with that of another is an easy trap to fall into here. This occurs when you use your own experience to claim an understanding of what someone else is going through. This is problematic for several reasons. When you bring your own experience into the conversation, you do two things: First, you stop listening to share, and second, you redirect or override the conversation to focus on yourself. Whether you intend to or not, you take away the impact of what someone is telling you and communicate that their experience isn't unique or as important as it feels to them at that moment.

For example, if someone is telling you about how their cat recently died and you, in response, tell them about how your cat died four years ago, are you being empathetic? Probably not. At the very least, you're not communicating your empathy effectively.

It's important to try to understand the other person's unique experience first. There may be a place or time, later, to share that you have some understanding or more ability to empathize because of your experience. However, this is different than making the conversation about you or prioritizing your own experience and minimizing theirs.

There's a key difference between trying to understand

and assuming how another person feels. This is the difference between listening to understand and listening selfishly. You also don't need to verbalize how you're able to empathize to be seen as displaying empathy; in fact, this is one of the significant misunderstandings about empathy in general. It's not about what you say. Keep in mind that the word "empathy" itself comes from the Greek word "pathos," which refers to emotion, not language.

Listen for Tone

Empathetic engagement involves deep listening. You need to gather as much information about the person's emotions as possible through listening to their words and intent, watching their body language, and, most of all, listening to the tone of their voice. The action of the muscles in our face and neck are directly affected by our emotions. Our throat constricts when we're upset, for instance.

Even more than these more obvious cues, smaller indicators in tone can transform the meaning of words from, for instance, a statement to an accusation. Anger is one of the easiest attitudes to read for most people, but it can sometimes be the case that other tones are mistaken for anger. Gaining a complete picture of what someone is trying to communicate also involves being aware of what they don't intend to share. If someone is frustrated or sad and trying to hide this, their body language and tone will give you clues and insight into what they might be experiencing.

Focus on the Speaker

Once you begin to grasp what someone is feeling, it's even more critical that you give them your full attention. When we're dealing with an emotional situation, or any situation that brings up emotions, our emotions tend to become more reactive. The other person may be more sensitive or volatile, too. This is simply the nature of emotions. They can even override rational thought.

People often dismiss considerations of emotion in daily interactions such as familiar workplace discussions. However, remaining attuned to emotional shifts and approaching every conversation with empathy will dramatically improve your ability to support those around you when they need it most. You may even discover there have been underlying emotional tensions you were unaware of or unconsciously making worse.

Consider Why the Message Is Important

If you're having trouble connecting with someone's emotions, it can help to think about why the message they're sharing is so important to them. You may not share a similar enough experience to connect with those emotions, and that's okay. Perhaps you simply don't understand why a situation is causing an emotional reaction that's different than expected or different from what you think you would experience in a similar situation. Whatever the reason, doing your best to place yourself in that person's shoes will help you begin to empathize and view the situation from their perspective rather than simply observe their emotions.

This technique is crucial because it's difficult to avoid commenting or passing judgment on emotions without causing conflict. This is also a way to catch yourself if you're slipping into judgment. When you feel the urge to question someone's emotions or reaction to their experience, take a moment to consider why you have that urge. Have you truly tried to empathize, or are you skipping straight to passing judgment? Did you truly listen to what they were saying, or are you using their sharing to reinforce your own stereotypes or preconceptions or to accomplish your own goals?

It's difficult to talk about empathy effectively because it's something you must experience to understand. While most humans are capable of empathy, it takes work, and it isn't always pleasant. That said, practicing the ability to more deeply understand one another is something that ultimately benefits us all.

Practical Tips

Emotions aren't something you can touch, so you might imagine that it's difficult to practice being empathetic. You'd be quite wrong. In fact, there are lots of ways to practice empathy, and this practice pays off. Becoming more empathetic can do more for you than just improving your ability to listen actively; it can have dramatic effects throughout your life and relationships. Because there are so many empathy practices readily accessible online, we'll focus on just one possible exercise here.

Even for someone who's already empathetic, engaging in an empathy exercise can be a valuable reminder of just how much work is involved in developing empathy; it might make you more empathetic toward someone who's struggling to learn empathy themselves (see what I did there?).

Perform Acts of Kindness

Once a day for the next three weeks, commit yourself to perform an intentional kindness toward someone. This can be a small thing, such as an encouraging text message, or it can be something more significant. Perhaps you plan to take someone out to a surprise dinner, for example. These acts don't need to have a specific cause or purpose, such as a birthday celebration—and they're often more impactful if they don't.

It's better if you're looking for ways to improve another person's day just because you can. You will, however, need to think about what type of kind act would mean the most to that person. A surprise dinner, for example, might be stressful for someone who works early the following morning. You'll need to think about how your actions impact that person. Simply performing these acts will help prompt your brain to develop the habit of considering how other people are feeling every day. As a result, it will become much easier to empathize with any person speaking to you.

CHAPTER 7: STEP 5 – BE PATIENT

Patience is difficult. There's no other word for it. Even for those more adept and experienced in exercising patience, it's rarely easy.

In practice, listening with patience is simple: don't interrupt. However, it's also one of the most challenging aspects of active listening. So, why is finding the patience to keep our mouth shut so hard?

Part of the answer might be that we're social creatures for whom engaging and interacting are reinforced throughout our lives. Keeping silent is difficult when we want to connect. So it's important to understand that, sometimes, to connect effectively requires us to let go of our need to share our perspectives, feelings, concerns, opinions, or ideas. This is the step where waiting becomes problematic. Patience and waiting to talk aren't the same.

For example, say someone is telling a story and seems to be spending far too long describing the details of the cabin where it all occurred. You cut in to ask what finally happened. They look a little taken aback and get to the point, and then leave immediately afterward. As it turns out, the cabin they were describing was one they built with their deceased father, so it's still tied to a lot of emotion for them.

By rushing their story, you conveyed that you weren't engaged in how they were telling it. Worse, you failed to pick up on their internal struggle because you didn't take the time to step back from your impatience and observe their tone and body language.

Waiting vs Patience

It's especially challenging not to interrupt when you

have a counter-argument in mind. That, in and of itself, should clue you in. Arguments require two. Rather than immediately trying to contradict the speaker's point with your own, try to empathize and consider the other person's perspective. Why might they feel the way they do or adopt a particular stance, for instance?

Even when engaging in a discussion, it's essential to allow the speaker to finish each point before asking questions. Why? Simple respect. Talking over someone or interrupting is about more than the content of the words; it's about what your actions convey. You're choosing to replace someone's words and thoughts with your own when you don't need to do so.

Think about why you're in such a rush to speak. Have you truly been listening to what the other person is saying? If they haven't completed their thought yet, the answer is no. Patience involves actively choosing to quiet your responses and sense of urgency.

Understandably, certain situations require that a

conversation be cut short. However, rushing someone to get to the point, or even speaking for them when it feels they aren't getting there fast enough, isn't only dismissive but often deeply hurtful.

Empathy

Someone struggling to get to the point is likely experiencing emotions or internal conflict not immediately apparent. They might even be working up the courage to broach an entirely unrelated subject. If you interrupt, you'll never know what they might have said or what you might have learned from it.

Actively practicing engaging in empathy might help you to quiet your impulses. Consider that the person might be uncomfortable for any number of reasons. They might still be working through a thought that's not yet fully realized.

When you speak for someone, you take away their voice and close the door on a potential opportunity for innovation or insight. Everyone's mind is different, and it's important not to assume yours knows best or understands what another mind is thinking. This form of arrogance and ego simply has no place in active listening.

As a practical technique, especially when you first begin working on listening patiently, walking yourself through the steps of focused attention is a great place to start. This not only reminds you why you're practicing patience but gives you specific aspects of listening to focus on and keeps your attention away from yourself and your desire to move the conversation along. Many people find that breathing exercises facilitate patience, too.

Practical Tips

Patience is a difficult skill to practice because doing so takes—you guessed it—patience. That said, there are some simple exercises that will help you build up your patience muscles. Over time, with practice, you'll be able to sustain patience over more extended periods. This, in turn, will allow you to engage in longer, deeper conversations.

Since being patient might mean enduring experiences that are challenging for you, you'll need to acknowledge that you'll continue to face difficult experiences. That's life. Improving your patience simply equips you to better navigate these inevitable frustrations.

Focus on Breathing

Any time you're hit with the desire to interrupt someone with an objection, take a breath instead. Follow this first breath with another, slower breath.

Ask Yourself Questions

Ask yourself why you want to control this situation. Once you have your answer, ask yourself if it's necessary to control the situation. Odds are, one or both of these answers will be no. Acknowledging this will help you to release the need to do anything except be patient.

Practice Disagreeing

Choose a TV show, documentary, podcast, or article that takes a stance you disagree with. Watch, listen to, or read this piece of media for 15 minutes. It's probably a good idea to set a timer. As you consume the media, keep the remote in your hand (or the equivalent).

Every time you disagree with something that's said or written, hit pause or look away from the text. Take a breath. Take another breath. Practice disagreeing without arguing by reminding yourself that there will always be opinions that aren't the same as your own. Wait until you feel calm and at peace with the piece of media that's presenting a different opinion than your own.

Now, go back to the media and repeat this process each time you have the urge to argue or push back against something you disagree with. A word of warning—this exercise is challenging. You'll likely get frustrated. The challenge for you is to continue performing this exercise for longer and longer periods of time. Each time, push yourself a little more.

CHAPTER 8: STEP 6 – BE RESPECTFUL

You've likely noticed that each of these steps ties back to respect. At its core, listening communicates respect for the speaker. You convey that you'll thoughtfully consider what's being said and that you respect the person speaking enough to allow them to speak without rushing or interrupting. This is most obviously challenging when you disagree with someone. However, respect is at play every time you engage in listening.

It's difficult to hide when you lack respect for someone

and almost impossible to listen effectively. That said, making the additional effort can speak volumes. It also provides an opportunity to stretch yourself and try to grow your capacity for patience. Unfortunately, failing to listen communicates a lack of respect, whether that's how you feel or not.

If you're paying attention to the message your voice and body are communicating to the other individual, you're more likely to catch yourself when you're tired or stressed and unable to listen well. You may explain the situation or request that the conversation be postponed to avoid insulting the other individual. Otherwise, you're likely to give the impression you don't respect them or what they have to say.

Think about a time you came away from a conversation feeling disrespected or belittled. It's likely those feelings resonated far beyond that interaction. Even patterns of dismissal in insignificant interactions can build into a deep resentment with a lasting impact on relationships. This is one of the few places where intent tends to matter less, in the moment, than the actual impression you're making.

Whether with silence or words, you can work to build rapport and trust through active listening. Essentially, this comes down to—almost—the classic saying: "Treat others in the way that you believe *they* would want to be treated." Note the key difference here. Not everyone wants to be treated as you would in a given situation. Everyone is different. Part of trying to empathize involves understanding that other people's experiences are unique to them. They want to be treated in specific ways. If you're actively listening, you should have a sense of what that means for them.

As tempting as it is to judge, remember that judgment is something you bring with you. It has nothing to do with the other individual as a person. It involves actively wanting to disprove, undermine, or dismiss what the other person is saying. This can be because of who's speaking, what they're saying, or how they're saying it. Be careful. Disagreeing is different than judging. You don't have to agree with someone to listen effectively.

This doesn't mean you should, or even can, abandon your own beliefs and opinions. It does mean that

93

you're choosing not to simply dismiss, shut down, or argue with what someone is saying. First, you're simply listening. Then, from the perspective of someone who's listened to not only what's being said but considered the intent and made an effort to empathize with the speaker, you can consider responding.

Even your response, however, should be grounded in respect. Do your best to remain neutral and nonjudgmental. Remember your role as a listener. You aren't present as an arguer or a convincer. Most often, the person talking to you simply wants to be heard. If they're truly interested in or want your opinion, they'll ask for it in most cases.

When talking about respect, we must also consider what it means to be supportive of someone. Listening well can involve supporting that person by responding, but this is entirely different than simply telling someone what they want to hear or agreeing just to agree. That isn't your job as a listener, either. In personal relationships, you might want to validate what someone is feeling, but even this isn't healthy when taken to an extreme. Communicating that someone's feelings or emotional experiences are valid differs from considering them right or correct. Making space for people to share their experiences requires an understanding of this critical distinction.

If you're listening to understand with empathy, there will naturally be times when you know that support is warranted and in a way that you can provide. Keep in mind that this shouldn't often happen. If it does, take a step back and consider whether you're falling into the common tendency to just agree because, for instance, it makes the conversation go more quickly or because you think you should. Remember that listening isn't about agreeing or disagreeing.

Practical Tips

Respect is important. You want to be respected, and the people you interact with every day—or even in passing—want the same. A simple, powerful exercise can help jumpstart your awareness of the role respect plays in your interactions.

Start a Respect Journal

Journaling isn't everyone's cup of tea; luckily, this exercise doesn't require you to commit to daily journaling. Instead, over the next two months, you'll simply be taking half an hour or an hour once a week to sit down and compose a journal entry. The point of this exercise isn't to get you to record your thoughts in a journal. In fact, if you want to simply sit and reflect on the relevant subjects rather than formally write them down, that's perfectly acceptable, too.

The goal is to set aside time to reflect on how you've demonstrated (or failed to demonstrate) respect for an individual through your interactions. At the end of each week, you select a different individual. Think back over your interactions with that person throughout the week. Consider your thoughts and behavior toward and in reference to that individual. Have you added anything to your interactions? Have you intentionally avoided that person or avoided telling them something? Have you told them something about another person that, by extension, shows disrespect for the other individual by betraying a trust? Have you been kind to them? Have you been dismissive of them or their ideas?

As the weeks pass, this task will become more and more complicated because you'll need to consider your interactions with people with whom you have a lesser (or closer) connection. Both can prove challenging. One week, you might need to reflect on an interaction with a stranger.

The purpose of this exercise is to prompt you to pay attention to how you're interacting with specific individuals—not in a single moment or interaction but as you go through your own ups and downs. For example, when we're tired or stressed, we might tend to let our baseline respectful treatment of others slip slightly. Taking the time to assess our behavior can reveal patterns in our conversations and interactions that we might not otherwise notice.

CHAPTER 9: STEP 7 – ASK QUESTIONS

In this chapter, we finally delve into the key element that distinguishes active listening from passive listening. While you can listen effectively without saying a word, this approach limits your ability to fully comprehend another person. You're limited to interpreting only what you're told. Active listening takes passive listening a step further by confirming that what you're told is the most complete and accurate version of the information, according to that individual.

While it's still just as necessary not to interrupt another person when they're talking to you, asking questions gives you several key benefits as a listener. First, it keeps you engaged. While various other techniques support attentive listening, asking questions based on the information you've just heard keeps you involved in the conversation, helps you stay focused, and even improves your memory about what's being discussed. Studies (Bugg 2012) show that asking questions forces your mind to process information in two ways—to help it become solidified in your memory and to make it more readily accessible and clear to you later.

In addition to improving your memory, asking questions provides you with more information and details about the subject under discussion. Let's take an obvious example. Consider, for instance, a case where a friend tells you they aren't feeling well. You might listen and even sympathize or give them a "get well soon" card. None of these options is wrong in and of itself; however, each one fails to dig into the cause of your friend not feeling well. What, after all, does "not feeling well" even mean? It could mean several things.

In fact, by failing to ask for more details, you might give the other person the impression that you're indifferent to or don't care about the causes of their upset. They might not be sick at all. Perhaps they aren't feeling well because they're nervous about a presentation, for instance. They might have fought with another friend and be feeling upset about that. Language—any language—is limited. The more detail you have to work with, the better you'll be able to understand what people are saying, why they're saying it, and how it impacts you and your actions.

In addition to body language and nonverbal cues, asking questions is the best way to demonstrate that another person has your attention. It's a signal of respect. You're telling the other individual that you care enough about what they have to say to want to know more. In fact, you may discover all sorts of new or relevant information that's even more meaningful, interesting, or worth exploring. Even if you don't, you've still provided the other person with the respect of trying to find out all you can about what they want to tell you.

It's important to make a distinction here. For anyone in a supervisory role, especially, it's tempting to want to use questions to keep a speaker on task or focused on what you want to talk about. By guiding the conversation in this way, you aren't only failing to listen actively, but you begin to not hear what the other person has to say as you plan your strategic questioning to get them to move toward a specific point. While in certain work-related situations, this can be an effective tool, it has no place in authentic active listening.

Jumping to a question or asking a question before the other person has had a complete opportunity to speak, however, is still just interrupting. When in doubt, don't. Or, at the very least, wait long enough to be certain that the other person is done speaking before asking your question. Every conversation has a natural ebb and flow, so it sometimes takes some practice to learn how to balance silence and questions. Keep in mind why you're asking a question; if you're asking because you need more information or more clarity, go for it. If you're asking just to ask or to sound like you're listening, you're missing the point.

You should also consider how easy it is to allow your mind to drift or not fully focus on what another person is saying. When you're actively listening and asking questions, you're keeping your mind on task. Even simple questions that clarify points or details that you think you understand or are making small assumptions about can help you here.

Depending on the situation, of course, your questions will vary dramatically. In certain circumstances, a specific question may be out of line or irrelevant. Still, it might be exactly the question to get you the information you need in another situation. These questions might be about anything, but to give you an idea of some of the basic approaches, consider these:

- When did that happen?
- Did this happen yesterday?
- How does that make you feel?
- Did this make you feel dismissed?
- Why is this important to you?

- Is this important to you?
- Where did you learn that?
- Did you learn that in school?
- Who was involved?
- Was [name of friend] involved?
- What do you want to do about that?
- Do you want to talk to them?

While these basic questions draw on the old standards of who, what, when, where, why, and how, they're a mix of the two basic types of questions—open-ended or closed-ended. After reading the following section, come back and see if you can determine which is which. You might even be able to make the distinction now.

Open-Ended vs Closed-Ended

There are, essentially, two types of questions. Wait, you might be thinking, didn't you just say there are basically infinite questions? Yes, the actual questions you can ask are essentially unlimited; however, all questions fall into one of two overall categories: open-ended questions and closed-ended questions.

Open-ended questions are questions that require an answer other than a simple "yes," "no," or "maybe." If it helps, you can think of them as long-answer questions because they demand more than a single-word response. These are the questions that will give you the most additional information and prompt the other person to do more than dismiss your question and move on. In general, open-ended questions encourage elaboration, whereas closed-ended questions provide specific information or clarification about a certain point. They're both useful in the correct context.

If someone is leaving out key details that are preventing you from understanding them entirely, it's important to prompt the speaker to elaborate. You might, in some cases, not even know that information is being left out until you ask. On the other hand, if someone is unclear, it's equally important to clarify what they're trying to say.

Sometimes, when clarity is particularly important or when you're trying to confirm that you understand a point that's been made, a closed-ended question might be the most effective approach. In general, however, closed-ended questions limit the amount of information you learn because you're shaping the question details rather than allowing the other person to shape the details of their response.

Whichever form of question you choose, keep in mind that how you ask it matters, too. Tone is vital in any conversation, as we've discussed, and it can dramatically impact how your questions are received. Think about how emphasizing a different word in these simple questions alters their meaning:

- **What** do you mean?
- What do **you** mean?
- What **do** you mean?
- What do you **mean**?
- You did **that**?
- You **did** that?
- **You** did that?

Do you hear the difference? Though these questions are simplistic, your diction (the words you choose and how you say them) is important, too. It's quite easy for questions to sound patronizing if they're overly simple, for instance, or condescending if they're needlessly elevated or didactic. Part of demonstrating respect for the person you're listening to is being conscious of and sensitive to their level and style of communication.

As we'll discuss in the reflective-listening chapter, matching your form or style of communication with the other person's can communicate that you're actively paying attention and trying to better understand where they're coming from.

Practical Tips

Most of us have a good grasp on how to ask a question; asking a question in a listening situation, however, can be more complicated. This is partly because, in addition to the details of the question itself, you're navigating how to break into someone else's dialogue without actually interrupting. Because of this, it's essential to practice asking active-listening questions intentionally. Practicing the questions themselves outside of this context won't help you much in this case. However, there are still strategies that can make this transition easier.

Start Small

For the next week, in each of your conversations, ask one open-ended and one closed-ended question. Even if you don't require clarification or elaboration, if you practice speaking these questions within a conversation, you'll become more comfortable with asking them. To start, simply confirm a time or date or another specific data point that someone has mentioned.

Start Familiar

When asking small questions—like those in the exercise above—base them on the information you're already comfortable with. When you have an understanding of the subject matter, it will be much easier for you to pay attention to the timing of the question. As someone is speaking, pay attention to subjects they bring up. When they start talking about a topic that you understand well or are already familiar with, you can begin to plan your question.

Start with Friends

Ask your first several prompting questions to a friend, but don't tell them you're practicing asking active-listening questions. Being already comfortable with this person lowers the stress level for you. As a bonus, if (and when) a question does come across awkwardly or interrupts the flow of your friend's story, you can simply explain what you're doing.

CHAPTER 10: STEP 8 – UTILIZE REFLECTION TO PROVIDE FEEDBACK

When you see the word "reflection," your first thought is probably of a mirror. Good news! You're off to a great start! One critical aspect of active listening is to reflect back to the other person what you're hearing and understanding regarding what they're saying. It's a crucial means of engaging with both them and the information they're giving you.

Reflecting is an extension of both questioning and nonverbal signaling. Done correctly, reflecting feedback to the person speaking signals that you hear and understand their words and their intent. Reflecting takes several different forms, and you're likely to use multiple variations within a single conversation.

Repeating Back

Also called reflective listening, this form of reflecting is self-explanatory. However, it's also quite easy to misuse. Repeating someone's words back to them allows both participants to hear those words again. It's an effective means for you to internalize the information and communicate to the speaker that you're following what they're saying. Generally, you won't be repeating full sentences, of course. You likely already do some variation of repeating naturally since this communication habit is a logical way to confirm that you comprehend meaning within an ongoing conversation.

In certain contexts, combining repeating with other techniques can communicate your respect for the speaker far better than silence. With children, especially, repetition is so vital to their learning and development that they rely heavily on it to sort out how you're feeling or engaging with what they're saying. Combining positive or encouraging body language cues—such as kneeling to get on their physical height level or simplifying your speech slightly—might be combined with simply repeating their words to communicate to a child that you care about what they have to say and want to understand them.

Even for adults, repeating is a means of telling the other person that you're attempting to "step into their shoes" and adopt their perspective so you can better understand it. You're conveying that you're trying to understand the words they're saying and, depending on your tone, communicating empathy for their feelings and thoughts about the subject they're talking about.

Repeating can be the trickiest reflecting tool to use effectively because overuse will instantly cause the other person to become distracted, angry, or even shut down altogether and discontinue the conversation. It's best used sparingly. Moreover, if speaking the words back out loud feels like it might interrupt the other person's train of thought, it's still a good technique to keep you mentally engaged. Making sure you can repeat the last few words of a key point can be a helpful tool to check yourself for distraction.

Mirroring

As in a physical mirror, this technique involves reflecting a speaker's words, feelings, and behaviors back to them. It's a great way to check that you've heard the other person's words accurately, particularly if there's a language barrier or other impediment. You are, essentially, using a language mirror to show the other individual what they've said and how they've said it.

Keep in mind that the goal isn't to imply that everything a person is saying is correct or accurate. Rather, you're communicating that you understand what the other person is saying. You'll be better able to respond, after all, when you do fully comprehend.

The other individual will also benefit from hearing their own words; they might realize they disagree with part of what they said or didn't intend the meaning conveyed by their choice of words. This provides them with the opportunity to clarify or make a correction. It's also a good way to catch yourself before hyper-focusing on a term or tone. The other person might self-correct, and what you thought would be a point of concern might be addressed for you.

As with repeating of words, it helps to restrict your mirroring to short snippets such as the final words of a sentence or an important point. Or, you might mirror a set of words that seems unclear, surprising, or unusual for the person to say in the given context. It can be a means of prompting more information, like in open-ended questioning, or receiving clarification, like in closed-ended questioning.

People will naturally pause to allow you to digest or process information. Mirroring helps communicate that you've followed the speaker's words to that point and encourages them to continue. With a few simple words that distract neither you nor the speaker, you can confirm the facts about their thoughts, feelings, and desires.

Be careful here: you can easily convey mockery, even without intending to, through mirroring. Remember that you aren't trying to impersonate the other individual—quite the opposite. You're encouraging and supporting them. Your level of connection with the other person will inform exactly how you employ mirroring.

Paraphrasing

Similar to repeating, paraphrasing or summarizing what a person has just said takes the process a step further. To effectively paraphrase, you must have understood what was said enough to draw out the key points. Generally, if your understanding is accurate, the statement will fit in with the speaker's line of thought. They'll ingest it subconsciously, without it interrupting their thought process. However, if you've misunderstood, this will jar them enough to address the disparity between what they want to communicate and what you understood.

Paraphrasing is a great way to confirm that what you think is the main point of what was said actually is the main point they intended. It's also an excellent way to train your mind to listen well and remain engaged; if your mind wanders, you won't be able to effectively sum up what someone has said. When you first begin to work on improving your active-listening skills, try to paraphrase for yourself every conversation you participate in. This doesn't need to happen out loud, especially not at first. Teaching yourself to process the speaker's information as you receive it and identify the critical points will keep you engaged in what they're saying and better equip you to respond.

Reflecting can easily lead to a deeper conversation because you're more actively involved as a speaker and more likely to bring your thoughts and opinions into the discussion. However, when you're actively listening, remember that the goal isn't to share your thoughts so much but to focus on the other person and use yourself as a mirror to amplify what they're saying.

In some situations, it might be even more impactful for the speaker to have their own words reflected back to them; this is a particularly effective means of countering negative self-talk, among other things. If someone is made to hear their own words—perhaps rephrased slightly for effect—they might begin to view those words differently.

Don't plan to simply throw this technique at every conversation and expect it to be effective, however. It can easily become frustrating for the person speaking if their words are simply being parroted back at them throughout an entire conversation. The purpose of reflecting isn't for you to serve as a wall that the other person's words bounce off of, after all. If you absorb their words, consider them, and then offer them back, you're far more likely to be engaging as an active listener.

Practical Tips

Because of the nature of reflective listening, group exercises are the most effective means of practicing this step. Unfortunately, you can't use an actual mirror to practice mirroring. Instead, you need to interact with at least one other individual. For those of you who are nervous about trying out these techniques on strangers or even friends, the good news is that you can use the television as a stand-in if you need to. The goal, especially at first, is to lower your stress level as much as possible so you can free up your full concentration to focus on repeating, mirroring, and paraphrasing.

Mirror Your Favorite Show

Choose a TV show or movie you like and have watched before. Try to find one that's live-action (rather than animated). The more extended-dialogue scenes there are, the better. The reason for opting for a television show or movie you happen to be familiar with already is that you won't be as distracted by the content. You already know what's going to happen, after all.

Instead, you can focus on a particular character. Each time this character is shown speaking to or facing the camera, you pretend they're talking to you. If they ask a question or pause between sentences, respond in some way. As they speak, think about how to mirror their posture and body language with your own body language, regardless of whether they're sitting or standing. You can still mirror when someone is standing and you're sitting, and you can practice as many variations of this as you like. When another character starts to speak, you can hit pause and practice paraphrasing what was just said as though in conversation with the character.

A single television show episode is a good choice for this exercise because it allows for a reasonable amount of practice within a set time limit. If you opt for a longer movie, set a timer for half an hour, and practice your reflecting within this timeframe. This exercise can be a lot of fun, so do try to have fun with it. The more comfortable you can get with responding to a screen, the lower the barrier to entry will appear when you begin to practice the same behavior with live people.

CHAPTER 11: STEP 9 – SEEK CLARIFICATION

Seeking clarification can be accomplished in multiple ways—often through a nonverbal prompting gesture. Think about any conversation you've had where someone asked you a question or wanted you to recall a past event; the odds are that this was accompanied by a hand gesture or facial expression indicating a lack of clarity and encouraging you to say more.

However, the most common means of receiving clarification is through asking clarifying questions. These might be either open-ended or closed-ended questions. They might involve some variation of the words spoken by the other person—which is also a type of reflecting. So, why is seeking clarification its own unique step in the active-listening process? Because it incorporates and is interconnected with every other step.

Simply put, it's too important to overlook. It's crucial to confirm that you understand what someone is saying to you any time you're listening, so a reminder to check this is essential. For example, it's quite easy to assume you understand the other person's meaning. The words might seem completely clear to you. This is one of the traps that active listening helps you avoid. By seeking clarification or confirmation of what you've understood, you remove the possibility of misunderstanding—or, at least, you dramatically reduce it.

Though you can use closed-ended questions for clarification, you'll likely need open-ended questions that encourage the speaker to provide more information. Assumptions tend to happen when less is said. With fewer words to interpret, your mind brings more of itself to them. What does this mean? Your brain is much more likely to apply your own relevant experiences, feelings, and memories and associate these with the other person's words. Your mind will do this regardless, though the more information the speaker provides, the fewer the gaps your brain will want to fill in with your own experiences and assumptions. How we perceive and process can have a dramatic and disastrous impact when we fail to clarify meaning.

For example, consider a friend telling you they're upset because they had to spend their weekend dealing with their basement flooding. If you've had experience with minor flooding—say, an inch or two of water in your basement in the past—you might easily believe you understand how upset they are. You're drawing on your similar experience to help you empathize. While empathy might help you understand some of what the other person is feeling and experiencing, you're also making an assumption that your two situations are similar. It's important to ask a clarifying question first.

Perhaps, when you ask how bad the flooding is, they

tell you there are several feet of standing water in the basement and that the foundation, plumbing, and electricity are compromised. Discovering they'll need to relocate to another living space puts their "upset" in a different context. While you might understandably have moved on from the flooding story after a brief commiseration based on your initial understanding, this new clarification might prompt you to completely different feelings and behavior. You might even offer to have your friend stay in your guest room or on your couch until things are sorted out. Note that the clarifying question, in this case, is open-ended. Were you to ask, "Was the flooding bad?" you might have received a yes or no answer that failed to clarify the issue.

Seeking clarification is as beneficial for you as it is for the person you're listening to. After all, that person wants to be heard and understood; it's generally safe to assume no one wants to be misunderstood when speaking to you, no more than you do when you're speaking to someone else.

Failing to clarify what someone is telling you creates

space for misunderstanding and resentment. It also communicates a lack of respect for the other person. If you truly care about what someone is saying, you'll make an effort to completely understand them rather than assuming and moving on based on your assumption.

As with reflecting, it's still important to wait for a pause to ask a clarifying question. After all, the speaker may provide the clarification themselves if you simply wait to hear it. You'll ask better, more pointed clarifying questions if you actively paraphrase. Paraphrasing will enable you to establish what you're taking away from what someone has said. Once you know your takeaways, you have a much better idea of where the gaps in your understanding are and are better equipped to see areas where clarifying will give you a more complete picture.

Practical Tips

Seeking clarification requires both recognizing that you don't understand something and admitting, to yourself and others, that you require help to fully comprehend it. This is the biggest stumbling block for many people learning the habits of active listening. It's challenging to admit that we need help, so asking for clarification can feel like weakness or failure.

Simply understanding that you need more information is just the first step. Once you know that you require clarification, things get trickier. This is where practicing asking for clarification comes in. As uncomfortable as it may feel to admit that you don't understand something, you won't learn more or grow if you don't ask for more details. A simple (yet challenging) exercise will get you on the road to becoming more comfortable asking for help.

Admit that You Don't Understand

This sounds simple enough, but you need to practice saying the words. Once a day for the next week, say to someone, "I don't understand," without apology or excuses. This might be the start of a longer sentence, such as, "I don't understand how to sharpen the lawnmower," but those first three words should be the same. This is, for many people, the most difficult part of getting comfortable asking for clarification. Specifically, you're admitting that you need help from another person. That can be hard, and it will continue to be difficult until it becomes more familiar.

During this exercise, it's also important to avoid placing blame as a way of sidestepping that uncomfortable feeling. For instance, saying, "I don't understand because you didn't explain clearly," isn't in the spirit of this exercise. Own your failure to comprehend. Start to recognize that not understanding something isn't a thorough assessment of you as a person. You aren't stupid or uneducated because you require clarification. Once you're over this roadblock, it will become easier to clearly articulate what you need help understanding. You'll also likely discover yourself being more patient when others require clarification from you.

CHAPTER 12: STEP 10 – SUMMARIZE

Summarizing is the final critical aspect of active listening. For longer periods of listening, you should periodically summarize out loud what you've heard. This is a good test of your understanding of the other individual's message. If your summary is slightly off-base, the speaker can correct it before you begin to add more information on top of that misunderstanding.

Essentially, summarizing enables both you and the other person to identify the most important parts of what was said—notably, you should also be able to identify what the speaker feels is most important, which might be slightly different than what you feel is their priority. Here are a few phrases that might help give you a sense of how to approach summarizing:

- "Let me confirm that I understand. First, ..., then ..."
- "Okay, on the one hand..., but on the other hand ..."
- "It sounds like ... and ... are important to you. Is that right?"
- "Do you think it's correct to say that you feel ...?"

Stopping to summarize provides you with a chance to synthesize all the information you've received, verbal and nonverbal, including information about the speaker's emotions. By doing so, you can connect key ideas and feelings to get a more complete picture of what was said. This, more than anything, prepares you to engage in quality conversation.

As part of active listening, the ability to summarize ties everything together. All your work to remain engaged and communicate your engagement, to empathize and clarify, are essentially wasted if, at the end of your conversation, you don't understand the most important aspects of what was said and how the speaker feels about those key points. Summarizing might feel redundant, but it matters. It will also help you recall your interaction more accurately in the future because it's much easier for your brain to latch onto your repetition of the key points than to try to sort back through the many words of the conversation after time has passed.

Of course, there are a few traps it's easy to fall into when summarizing. The first is editorializing. A summary shouldn't be your commentary on what the other person said but rather a condensed or boiled-down version. This isn't the place for you to bring your own opinions or feelings into play; that can come later, if appropriate. First, you need to ensure you fully understand what's been said. Otherwise, you may be passing judgment based on inaccurate or incomplete understanding, leading to mutual frustration.

Be on the alert for your tendencies (we all have them) to bring your own desire to fix, judge, or redirect onto yourself. When summarizing, it's tempting to want to diagnose or "fix" a perceived problem or offer advice or suggest what the other person should do. Keep in mind that none of this is part of active listening. Remember, for now, you're only listening. Release some of your desire to control and simply allow yourself to get as close to experiencing what the other person is experiencing as possible.

Practical Tips

It's much more difficult to summarize what someone has said than to write a formal summary of a text for the simple reason that it's impossible to visually review what someone has said. All that you have left after someone has spoken is your memory of what they were saying. Holding this information in your mind—especially if the person speaking happens to be particularly long-winded—is a challenge in and of itself.

Consolidating that information, sorting out the key points, and articulating those points is a process that takes quite a bit of experience to do well. Even great listeners often struggle with being able to effectively summarize what someone has told them. However, you can absolutely learn to summarize well. Once you do, this will become a powerful tool in your active-listening toolbox. The biggest stumbling block for many people is that they begin responding to the information before fully summarizing it.

Summarize Audio Clips

A great way to practice summarizing is with a podcast or other audio clip or audio narration. To begin, play the audio for a timed 10 minutes. At the end of that time, write down a three-sentence summary of the information. Then, identify the most critical point or piece of information that was given. Repeat this exercise every day for three weeks. Use a different piece of media each day (basically, don't just use consecutive clips of the same podcast).

Some audio clips will be much more challenging to summarize than others. Some you may have to listen to again to summarize well. However, you'll discover that, over time, your brain will begin to retrain itself to process the information it's hearing differently. It will begin to listen more closely and store key points in short-term memory to be more readily accessed.

Don't Add Anything

At least once a week, make a point to summarize what someone has just told you back to them. You can tell them what you're doing, or not, as you prefer. What you should focus on, however, is not adding any new information, insights, or opinions to your summary. There should be nothing added to what they spoke about. This is difficult. We all have opinions. Often, we simply want to support and help others. However, the ability to reflect and ensure that we fully understood someone's message must be the first step before we can hope to add anything valuable or worthwhile.

CHAPTER 13: VALIDATION

"Communication works for those who work at it."-
John Powell

Active listening is hard. Although we've broken down this process into 10 steps to help you access each component, these steps are interconnected. It's often difficult to know when you're failing at one step or when you should be applying a particular approach in a listening situation.

The good news is that this will come with time. You *will* improve. You'll need to practice, of course, and you'll make mistakes. That's okay! Far more important is making the effort. After all, we've taken a deep dive into what active listening looks like and the effort it requires, but it's important to remember your motivation for learning to actively listen in the first place.

When you actively listen, you receive information differently. Not only do you increase your odds of obtaining more accurate information, but you also process this information as it's given to you, synthesize and integrate it with what you understand about the person speaking, and, ultimately, get a much clearer picture of what's being said. This skill will consistently improve your listening and understanding and improve your critical thinking skills as you apply them in your everyday life.

This clarity of information is invaluable in the workplace. You'll save time because you won't be operating based on compounded misunderstandings, so you can keep your coworkers or team on the same page more easily. You'll likely notice a dramatic improvement in inter-office communication and in your ability to understand and accomplish the work you're assigned.

Whether the nature of the communication is platonic or romantic, this accurate information and understanding are just as valuable to maintaining trust in your relationships. As you learn to listen actively, you'll become a much better communicator. When you begin hunting for what's important to someone when they're speaking to you, you internalize how to communicate the things that are important to you.

Take some time now to consider which of the 10 steps involved in active listening are likely to prove most challenging for you. Look back through these chapters and the examples for each to help you consider how you can accomplish each step:

- Step 1: Focus Your Attention
- Step 2: Show that You're Listening
- Step 3: Listen to Understand
- Step 4: Listen with Empathy
- Step 5: Be Patient
- Step 6: Be Respectful

- Step 7: Ask Questions
- Step 8: Utilize Reflection to Provide Feedback
- Step 9: Seek Clarification
- Step 10: Summarize

Think about a few of your recent conversations and how you listened in each. Identify any patterns or habits that emerge in those memories. Ask someone you trust what they notice about your listening, too. Focusing on the areas where you'll benefit the most from immediate improvement will help you focus your energy.

Now, make a plan. Applying these practices in your life requires taking practical steps to implement and maintain them. For each, consider the behavior you must change to support your efforts to listen more actively. You may need to change how you approach someone if you're about to have a difficult conversation. You may need to change where you choose to have a conversation, too.

Active listening isn't easy or simple at first, but you can learn to do it well. Breaking the process down and working on improving only one or two of these critical steps at a time will help you build up sustainable habits of positive listening and communication. Trying to tackle them all at once is a recipe for disaster and unnecessary disappointment. Set yourself up for success, and you're far more likely to succeed in instituting lasting, positive changes in your life built upon healthier communication.

I want you to succeed. As you begin to work on your listening habits, you'll need to remind yourself how to listen well even as you listen. The danger here is becoming so distracted by the process that you fail to listen or stop listening altogether. Instead, be patient with yourself. Pay attention to when you've accomplished specific steps well and appreciate the outcome. You might even think about rewarding yourself in some small way as a form of positive reinforcement of your good listening behavior.

You don't need to enroll in a communication-theory course to understand how to listen well. You already have all the tools you need to begin improving your listening skills. Everyone must start somewhere; you might be quite surprised to discover that there are elements of active listening in which you already excel.

Through a combination of nature, development, and experience, each individual is more or less attuned to certain aspects of the listening process. While you're working on deepening your listening by adding more steps to those more comfortable for you, don't be afraid to lean into your areas of strength. Rely on the aspects of listening you do well so you can continue to grow without becoming overwhelmed by the process. Remember, if you're trying, you're already on the right course!

CONCLUSION

You chose this book because you want to improve your relationships and professional productivity. With a thorough understanding of the essential steps involved in the listening process, you're well on your well to accomplishing that goal. All that remains is to apply these skills in your everyday life and interactions.

Not only do you now better comprehend the psychology behind listening and how it factors into healthy communication, but you understand how breakdowns in listening negatively impact that communication. You've learned how to:

- Focus your attention
- Provide signals that you're listening
- Aim to understand
- Empathize with the speaker
- Increase your patience
- Practice respect
- Ask good questions
- Offer feedback
- Clarify meaning
- Summarize the message

With these 10 simple steps, you have the keys to becoming a better listener and, as a result, a more engaged and productive person.

Deep listening doesn't happen overnight, however. Cultivating this new mindset requires challenging your existing one and working to eliminate the habits that stand in the way of healthy communication.

You'll need to choose to confront the barriers that you've unconsciously established and the comfortable patterns of shallow listening that are standing in your way. The upside is that, once you do, these new habits will be just as robust and will stick with you through a lifetime of engaged listening. Challenging each of your negative habits, one by one, is a proven method of reshaping your entire mindset regarding listening.

Though the psychology is complex, the practical aspects of listening are, ultimately, simple. You want to eliminate the frustration and tension fracturing your relationships and bogging down your productivity. The good news is, you're already well on your way. We imagine you'll be recommending this book to quite a few friends, too, now that you're more sensitized to those unhealthy listening habits that they've developed and display to you.

Even if you don't share this book with them, you and your friends will benefit from your improved ability to communicate well and minimize the frustrations caused by miscommunication and misunderstanding. Deep listening is an effective way of leading you into deeper empathy, too, which those around you can't fail to notice.

Our job in this book was simple: To break down the overwhelmingly concept of active listening into manageable steps. Your job will be more difficult: Incorporate those elements into your daily life and work to understand those around you at a deeper level.

Don't be shocked to discover newfound levels of trust and compassion emerging within your many different relationships. Enjoy engaging as a healthier partner, leader, friend, and even parent. The result is well worth the effort. Now, what are you waiting for? Go out there and listen!

One more thing

If you enjoyed this book and found it helpful, I'd be very grateful if you'd post a short review on Amazon. Your support does make a difference, and I read all the reviews personally so I can get your feedback and make this book even better. I love hearing from my readers, and I'd really appreciate it if you leave your honest feedback.

Thank you for reading!

BONUS CHAPTER

I would like to share a sneak peek into another one of my books that I think you will enjoy. The book is titled _**"How to Make People Like You and Do What You Want: The Miracle Formula for Magnetic Charisma, Making People Laugh, and Exerting Influence."**_

Do you make your first impressions count? What if I told you that how you come across during the first 30 seconds of meeting new people affects nearly 85% of your relationships? What if I told you that the person you like takes only a split second to decide whether they like you or not. Doesn't it sound scary? That's because it is!

Whether you are pitching a product or idea to clients, preparing for a new job interview, or seeking to make great connections with the people you meet, your **"first interactions" are the most CRITICAL of all**. Just imagine. The countless hours spent talking, networking, and building relationships, those initial 30 seconds determine the majority of your success!

As adults, we tend to have less exposure to new potential friends than we did as children. During our childhood, we continuously met new kids through school, hobbies, sports, or just on the neighborhood's playgrounds. And the simple act of being in the same place repeatedly created bonds and friendships for many. In adulthood, most of us have lost those arenas. And even when we do spend time in public with other adults, we hardly ever interact with them in any meaningful way that might lead to more than – at best - a superficial conversation. Many of us are unsure of how to approach someone new and spark engaging conversations. We have become a population of adults who spend time *around* each other – but not *with* each other.

In this book, you'll learn simple and easily understandable techniques and tactics that will help you to confidently start exciting conversations, turn acquaintances into friends, and charm all you come in contact with.

Would you like to become more popular? Would you like to be able to socialize with people successfully? Would you like to improve your relationships? Would you like to be more of an extrovert? Would you like to have more friends?

Then this book is for you! In this book, we'll explore the social skills you need to become charismatic, more popular, more authentic, more confident, and a more appealing person!

You deserve to become the best version of yourself! You deserve to be more sociable and able to meet new people without getting nervous or anxious. You deserve to be confident! You deserve to have boundless self-esteem! You deserve to have great

149

relationships! You deserve to have many friends!

This book will teach you how to:

- Develop social skills to make new acquaintances, spread your influence, and increase personal power
- Convey and read body language to exude confidence, positivity, and strength
- Increase your popularity and extend your social network
- Make a striking and memorable first impression
- Develop communication skills, such as listening, interacting with individuals and groups, telling stories, and the art of persuasion
- Become an effective listener to establish deep connections and detect people's needs, desires, and motives

You've been misled about social skills. Most people make them out to be a rare, God-given gift that you're either born with or not. However, anyone can learn social skills. It is the same as learning a new sport or skill. Anyone can become socially successful as long as they are dedicated and follow proper strategies.

This book is for people who would like to develop better social skills & communication skills in any category of your life - work, family, or personal life. If you are socially shy, no problem, we will start from the basics to improve your social skills. If you already have good social skills, I'll share many advanced concepts & tips so you can develop even more extraordinary social skills.

You will learn how to make killer first impressions, how to remove your fear of approaching, how to connect with people, how to make friends, how to be confident & comfortable in any social setting, and how to be the most appealing person in the room.

Enjoy this free chapter!

In our daily lives, we meet and greet thousands of people. Some are just passers-by who happen to cross our path, while others make a strong impact on us. It's as if they craft an instant impression on our mind and heart—a quick memory woven into the fabric of our being. These people don't need to do too much or talk too much to stand out. They mesmerize and charm whoever they meet.

They can steal the light from anyone—no matter who they are. You can find such people everywhere around you, and chances are you were thinking of a few names as you read the last few lines. These people aren't celebrities or necessarily famous, but there's something about them that fascinates people. They can sway people's thinking and convince them with the slightest of expressions and minimal words.

Whether they're just strutting down the street, delivering a passionate speech in a room full of executives, talking to a colleague at the coffee shop, or sitting quietly in a boisterous swarm of people, there's something about them that sets them apart. It doesn't take them long to make friends with those around them because their magnetic and charismatic appeal pulls in and delights anyone who comes in contact with them.

When a person develops control over how people around them react to their words and actions, they can maneuver and manipulate their way through many situations. The slightest bit of confidence and amiability can get you through a ton of challenges in life. So, it doesn't come as a surprise that people who have well-developed social skills, leadership qualities, confidence, and tactics for dealing with people are always on the upswing in both their professional careers and personal lives.

Who doesn't want to be such a person? A person who walks into the room and everyone turns to look at them, a person who's the life of the party, a person who says a lot with just a few words, a person who's invited to every social gathering, a person who can gather a crowd around them regardless of where they are, a person who can keep their cool even when the situation tenses up, a person who can be humorous, a person who's adored by many and always consulted for advice, a person who's always the priority for anything and everything.

Their hands don't go clammy when they're thrust into an unfamiliar situation, their heart doesn't run wild when they're called upon to speak, their tongues don't become tied when their words are met with criticism or snide remarks, they're not interrupted by anyone in the group, they aren't the last to get picked for a team or the final choice for a promotion, and they aren't afraid to strike up a conversation with a complete stranger.

Do you wish to be such a person? Then you must begin by cultivating certain qualities. Developing this set of qualities will require practice and breaking the chain of your old habits. You'll need to work on yourself day and night to be a better version of yourself who isn't afraid to make mistakes.

People start to develop personality traits from an early age. Children are commonly referred to as sponges because they pick up everything that's happening around them. They might reproduce the personality traits or characteristics of their parents, siblings, friends, or even characters in cartoons they watch or books they read. These traits are practiced repeatedly by the child until they're hardwired into the child's brain and become habits. If they become accustomed to being in isolation, that's also something they'll be more comfortable doing later in life.

With most people, habits are unconscious. They don't think before they perform a particular action; they just do it. It's like breathing: You don't think about breathing. You just breathe. Similarly, you don't think about creating or acting from habit. You're so accustomed to doing something that the action is unconscious.

If you want to be a better version of yourself—one who has significantly higher social capital, is a better leader, and is great at relationships, outgoing, fully confident, and has a lot of friends—you'll need to break the cycle of your current habits to make space for new ones. You won't only achieve your goals of becoming more social and charismatic, but you'll also develop qualities that will ensure prosperity in your relationships and work.

In this book, we'll discuss the myriad of qualities you need to make part of your personality, and we'll explore the process of how to do this. We'll discuss the day-to-day situations that all of us face and how to respond to them. We'll share tips, tricks, and activities to ensure that newer, better traits replace your habits.

First of all, we'll conduct an in-depth personality analysis. You can't begin to change yourself and your habits if you don't know what they are. By answering a set of questions, you'll start to gain a better understanding of yourself. Self-knowledge is the hurdle between you and your best self—which is inherently charismatic and magnetic. So, take out a journal or a piece of paper and answer the following questions:

- If I were to describe myself in three words, what would those words be?
- What are my goals/aspirations?
- What does my ideal life look like?
- What brings me absolute joy and satisfaction?
- What are the things that make me unique?

- What do I consider to be my strengths?
- What do I consider to be my weaknesses?
- What fears are holding me back?
- What are my most recurring emotions?
- What do I value most about myself and the world around me?
- How do others view me?
- What do others value most about me?
- Am I offering substantial value to those connected to me in my work, or do I have more to bring to the table?

Once you pinpoint what situations and traits are challenging to you and why, you'll know what shortcomings have arisen in your journey to becoming a magnetic individual.

You'll need the answers to these questions to decide the best approach for changing your habits. This approach includes how to hone your social skills, how to build stronger relationships, how to work on yourself, how to build your self-esteem, how to be more confident, how to read people and their body language, how to become more popular, and how to become a better listener, among other things. We'll also talk about developing a strong presence, making brilliant first expressions, small talk, body language, correspondence and hand movements, words and their impact, and how to be a more influential person in general. You can expect to learn about how to control and handle anxiety, stress, and pressure. You can also expect to learn a few tricks about time management and building habits from the ground up.

Before we begin, here's a word of encouragement: Don't give up. A lot of people have been exactly where you are now. Some have given up and gone back to being completely invisible, living in the shadows of those around them. Others have taken this journey as a challenge and cast themselves in the brightest of colors, setting themselves apart from everyone.

Here's your chance to hand-pick a vibrant color for yourself and wear it ferociously so that you, too, can become a leader among your peers. You'll no longer be a bystander; your walk will cause those around you to gravitate toward you. I can assure you that by the end of this book, you'll have a plethora of tricks up your sleeve that will aid you in making more friends and achieving all your goals. However, the key thing here is practicing the strategies, being consistent, and not giving up. You need to strengthen your willpower. You can do so by constantly setting reminders for yourself, whether about practicing a new quality or making time to relax. Create reminders around the house—whether this be by using a clock, alarm on your laptop, or even on your refrigerator. Write down what you want to practice on a piece of paper and stick it to the mirror in your bathroom, the closet of your bedroom, or the steering wheel of your car. The point is to place your reminders where you'll see them often.

On this journey, you'll make mistakes and falter along the way. But the key to success is to get up, dust yourself off, and keep going. You never know if victory is just around the corner! Yes, you'll embarrass yourself at times. Yes, you won't achieve gold on your first attempt, but you'll eventually get there. These techniques are proven to give you an edge on those around you. So, what are you waiting for? Your new life—full of friends, family, relationships, happiness, and success—awaits you! Embrace it with open arms!

The Importance of Social Connections

Due to the nature of today's society, most of our day-to-day activities require that we be interactive. They require us to connect with those around us and make friends. Humans weren't created to remain isolated like islands. There's evidence of this from the earliest of times. Early societies traveled in groups—not only because of the power in numbers but also because activities like hunting, setting up a shelter, and other tasks were made easier through a cooperative effort.

Moreover, from the day a child is born, it develops connections and relationships with those around it. It's hardwired to connect with people and becomes profoundly social from a young age. We're drawn to those who help us, admire us, lead us, and take an interest in us. The impact of your first relationships reverberates throughout your life. If children are loved and taken care of from birth, they learn how to develop strong connections with others and thus are more likely to continue this pattern throughout life.

We're inherently, biologically, cognitively, physically,

160

and spiritually social creatures. There's no denying that. However, in the world we live in today, interacting with others and maintaining social connections can be challenging due to a variety of factors. Anxiety, stress, depression, and low self-esteem are a few leading contributors; they prevent people from putting themselves out there. If you answered the previous set of questions, you should be able to identify what holds you back when it comes to having valuable social connections.

Many people tend to isolate themselves or avoid social contact without weighing the negatives of doing so. Social connection is as essential for the health of the human body as eating a balanced diet, getting enough sleep, or exercising regularly. When you interact with those that bring joy and peace into your life, your brain releases feel-good hormones like dopamine and oxytocin, which instantly improve your mood and elevate the state of your brain and body. Certain hormones remove tension from your muscles and create a sense of well-being.

While it's true that social engagement helps improve a

person's emotional, physical, and mental health, it's also true that the lack of positive social involvement can have detrimental effects. Hence, one should always focus on the quality of their friendships rather than the quantity. For example, if you wanted someone in your life that you can rely on or celebrate with, you wouldn't call the person you talked to once at a conference; you're likely to call a close friend. That's the very essence of social connections. It's the sense of closeness or belonging you feel with an individual or a group of people. A study conducted by Pavey, Greitemeyer, and Sparks in 2011 proved through strong scientific evidence that social connection is one of the core psychological needs of any individual.

Happiness is contagious; it spreads through social connections. The positive attitude of the company you keep will rub off on you.

What Do People Look for in Friendships?

Here are a few key factors that people look for when seeking meaningful and gratifying friendships.

Trust

People with whom you share a strong bond feel comfortable enough to give you their honest opinion and offer constructive criticism. They aren't afraid to hurt your feelings. If you don't know someone well, they'd be reluctant to offend, so either their opinion will likely be sugar-coated or disingenuous. Accurate advice can only be gained from those who trust you and vice versa.

Respect

Respect is a broad term that includes everything from respect of another person's boundaries and values to respect for you as a person—what you stand for, what you do, what you believe in, and respect for those around you. Without the presence of respect, no relationship can work.

Acceptance

Those with whom you have a genuine friendship or relationship accept you. They don't try to negate you or ask you to change things about yourself that constitute who you essentially are. They welcome you as you are. They provide you with companionship that makes you feel more socially accepted in a larger group. When they accept you, you begin to discover common ground and become more comfortable with them.

Unconditional Support

The support provided by genuine relationships shouldn't come at a cost. It shouldn't be based on bargaining: "If I'm doing this for you, you have to do that for me." Rather, it should be, "You need help, so I'm here." No hesitation, just support without any conditions. Support helps you feel less lonely. You have people with you in your best times and your worst times. You're motivated by these people to do better and be better. When you're caught in a pickle, you can turn to them without thinking twice.

Obstacles to Healthy Relationships

There are a ton of factors that hinder people in developing stronger relationships. These include the stress and anxiety of approaching someone we don't know, the presence of cliques, the distractions of social media, working 24/7, not valuing other people enough, and much more. The lack of social connection can isolate a person from the rest of the world. When a person is alone, they're likely to become consumed by their thoughts and overthink everything. Overthinking is a key trigger for negative thoughts to brew.

Negative thoughts translate into negative actions and exuding a negative vibe. People tend to distance themselves from those who are negative and pessimistic. Being a victim of your mind will also make your self-esteem plummet. You won't feel enthusiastic about anything. The tiniest change around you can send you into a downward spiral. Your judgment will be clouded, and you'll make skewed decisions that will impact your personal and professional life.

Suffering defeats left and right takes a toll on our physical health. People who feel isolated often find unhealthy coping mechanisms to fill the void when social connections collapse. These might include overeating or overspending to get a temporary high or alcohol or substance abuse.

Social connection keeps a person grounded. It keeps them in touch with reality. They're aware of what's happening around them. They can make valuable connections that can help them climb the ladder of professional or personal success. Being connected socially pushes them to be a better version of themselves. We tend to have a positive outlook on life when we're surrounded by positive people.

The Benefits of Strong Social Connections

Much like our relationship with ourselves, good relationships with others are conducive to happiness and fulfillment, providing meaning and purpose in our lives. When you have positive relationships, you inundate your life with love and admiration, and you feel better about yourself. You feel worthy, valuable, and that you belong. A person who feels good about themselves brews positivity. They maintain a positive outlook on life and are ready for any challenge that life throws at them, which means they're prepared to face anything. Having strong relationships also gives you a sense of security. It's like a cushion you can always fall back on—a cushion of unconditional support and love.

Physical Health

Just as exercising can benefit your physical health, so can spending time with those you love. Positive social connections can help reduce stress and increase cardiovascular health. Additionally, studies have shown that social interactions can lead to a more robust immune system.

Mental Health

Interacting frequently with others improves your cognitive functions. Your brain becomes sharper. The more you hang out with someone, the more characteristics you can identify about them. You understand how they deal with people, react in different situations, and handle life in general. Participating in social activities can also help your mental health by reducing depression and anxiety. It can lighten your mood and make you feel happier. Additionally, suicide, mental illness, and alcoholism rates are much lower in people who feel a sense of belonging.

Get your full copy today! *__"How to Make People Like You and Do What You Want: The Miracle Formula for Magnetic Charisma, Making People Laugh, and Exerting Influence."__*

BOOKS BY RICHARD BANKS

How to be Charismatic, Develop Confidence, and Exude Leadership: The Miracle Formula for Magnetic Charisma, Defeating Anxiety, and Winning at Communication

How to Stop Being Negative, Angry, and Mean: Master Your Mind and Take Control of Your Life

How to Deal with Grief, Loss, and Death: A Survivor's Guide to Coping with Pain and Trauma, and Learning to Live Again

How to Deal With Stress, Depression, and Anxiety: A Vital Guide on How to Deal with Nerves and Coping with Stress, Pain, OCD and Trauma

The Positive Guide to Anger Management: The Most Practical Guide on How to Be Calmer, Learn to Defeat Anger, Deal with Angry People, and Living a Life of

Mental Wellness and Positivity

Develop a Positive Mindset and Attract the Life of Your Dreams: Unleash Positive Thinking to Achieve Unbound Happiness, Health, and Success

The Keys to Being Brilliantly Confident and More Assertive: A Vital Guide to Enhancing Your Communication Skills, Getting Rid of Anxiety, and Building Assertiveness

Personal Development Mastery 2 Books in 1: The Keys to being Brilliantly Confident and More Assertive + How to be Charismatic, Develop Confidence, and Exude Leadership

Positive Mindset Mastery 2 Books in 1: Develop a Positive Mindset and Attract the Life of Your Dreams + How to Stop Being Negative, Angry, and Mean